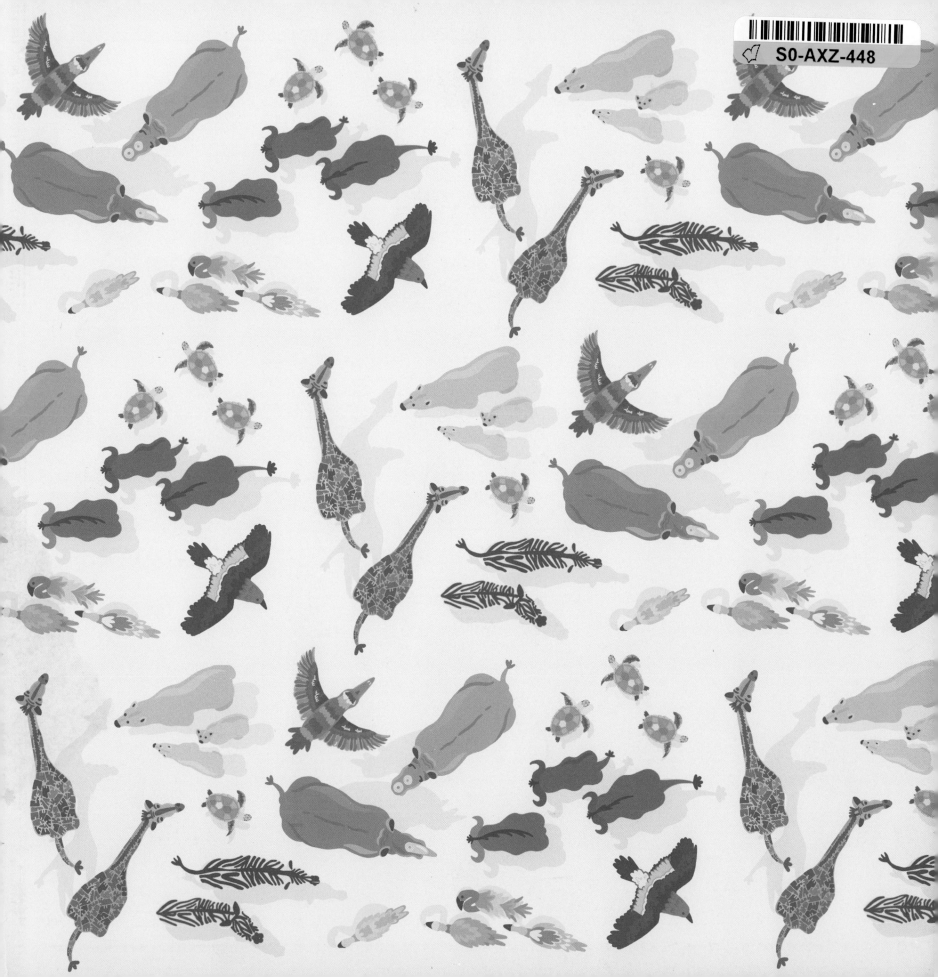

LOOK DOWN AND SEE

NATURAL WONDERS
OF THE WORLD

BETHANY LORD

First published in the UK in 2019 by

Ivy Kids

An imprint of The Quarto Group

The Old Brewery

6 Blundell Street

London N7 9BH

United Kingdom

www.QuartoKnows.com

A CIP record for this book is available from the Library of Congress.

ISBN: 978-1-78240-921-2

This book was conceived, designed & produced by

Ivy Kids

58 West Street, Brighton BN1 2RA, United Kingdom

PUBLISHER   David Breuer

MANAGING EDITOR Susie Behar

ART DIRECTOR   Hanri van Wyk

DESIGNER   Bethany Lord

IN-HOUSE DESIGNER Kate Haynes

ASSISTANT EDITOR Lucy Menzies

Text by Susie Behar

Manufactured in Guangdong, China TT072019

1 3 5 7 9 10 8 6 4 2

MIX
Paper from
responsible sources
FSC® C016973

LOOK DOWN AND SEE
NATURAL WONDERS
OF THE WORLD
BETHANY LORD

IVY KIDS

CONTENTS

INTRODUCTION

There are many amazing places to see in the world, and many ways in which to see them. You can look at photographs, see them in movies or on TV, or visit them in person. But have you ever seen a world-famous wonder from a bird's-eye view? This means looking directly down on it from a height. Everything looks very different—as you will find out when you turn the pages of this book. It will be a spectacular trip. You are going to see some of the most wonderful sights in the world, as if you were a bird flying high above them. Since birds see things very differently from us, we've used our imagination to show a picture of what they could be seeing. So, some things will appear relatively larger than in real life.

The dot on the map shows you the location of each natural wonder.

The magnifying glass tells you to look carefully at the picture and to spot or count things.

North America

South America

Europe

Africa

Asia

Australasia

-LOFOTEN-

This group of small and large islands in **Norway** lies above the icy **Arctic Circle**.
There's an exciting wilderness of mountains, forests, sandy beaches, and
rocky sea inlets to explore. Visitors can look for moose and otters, see lively
puffin colonies, and watch majestic sea eagles swooping across the bays.
Most of the islands are connected by bridges or undersea tunnels,
but some of them can only be reached by boat. From the end of
May until mid-July, the sun never sets—it's light through the night!

*Soccer players can enjoy stunning
sea views. Lofoten's only field is
almost as wide as the rocky
island it is perched on.*

Look closely at the
picture. How many
boats can you count?

Many of the islanders make their living by fishing. In winter the sea is full of Arctic cod. These large fish gather here to breed.

The wingspan of the white-tailed sea eagle can measure almost 8 feet! This huge raptor hunts fish, smaller water birds and small mammals.

Lofoten's roads run over bridges and through undersea tunnels that connect the different islands.

North America

South America

Europe

Asia

Africa

Australasia

Every year, an enormous herd of wildebeest crosses the Mara River in search of fresh grass to eat on the plains of the Serengeti in **Tanzania, East Africa**. It is astonishing to see the wildebeest thundering through the river, kicking up waves of muddy water. These huge antelopes aren't the only animals making this trip. More than two million wildebeest, zebras, and gazelles move together through the Serengeti and Masai Mara national park in one vast migration.

People travel from all over the world to see the sight of this incredible animal migration—but it's only safe to watch if you're inside a vehicle!

Look closely at the picture. How many zebras can you spot among the wildebeest?

Wildebeest are powerful animals. Male adults can weigh 550 pounds and run as fast as 49 mph!

Running with the wildebeest herd helps to protect zebras from attack by predators, such as lions or crocodiles.

Small, colorful malachite kingfishers swoop low over the river hunting for fish and insects in the water.

North America

South America

Europe

Asia

Africa

Australasia

- THE - GRAND CANYON

This enormous canyon found in **Arizona,** in the **Southwest,** is 277 miles long, 18 miles wide and almost 1 mile deep. It is six million years old, and for thousands of years, the canyon and land around it was home to Native American communities. Today, it's a world-famous national park with millions of visitors every year. You can explore the canyon by helicopter, on foot, by canoeing along the river snaking along its floor, or simply by taking in the awesome view from a hanging skywalk bridge—scary!

Look closely at the picture. Can you see the faraway boats, the different colored rocks in the canyon wall and the birds flying overhead?

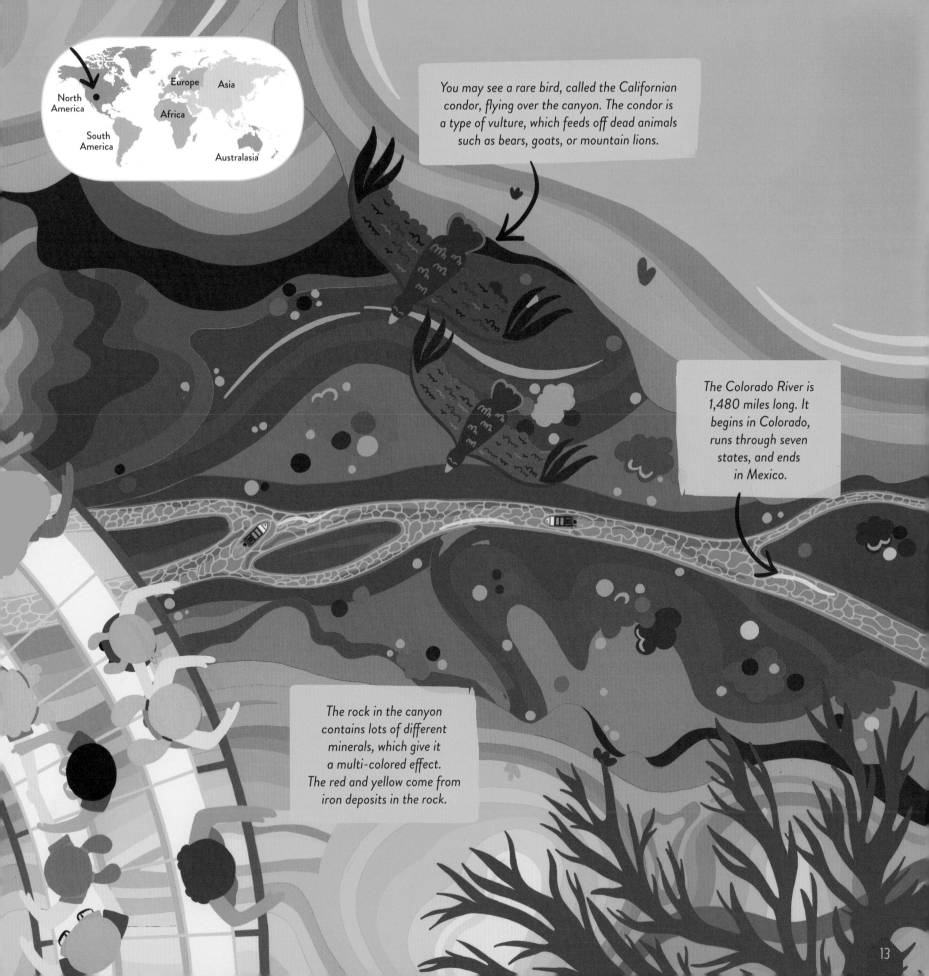

You may see a rare bird, called the Californian condor, flying over the canyon. The condor is a type of vulture, which feeds off dead animals such as bears, goats, or mountain lions.

The Colorado River is 1,480 miles long. It begins in Colorado, runs through seven states, and ends in Mexico.

The rock in the canyon contains lots of different minerals, which give it a multi-colored effect. The red and yellow come from iron deposits in the rock.

North America

South America

Europe

Africa

Asia

Australasia

· VICTORIA · FALLS

This spectacular waterfall crosses two African countries, **Zambia** and **Zimbabwe**. It is immense—1 mile wide by 354 feet high. The Falls have another name: "The Smoke that Thunders." The booming of rushing water can be heard up to 24 miles away. Visitors can see the Falls from a helicopter or trek the trails high above them. They can swim in the pools or kayak along the river below the waterfall. The nearby national parks are home to crocodiles, elephants, buffaloes, giraffes, zebras, and lions, and you may even spot a cheetah.

The African fish eagle swoops down to snatch fish from the water with its sharp talons. This large bird's wingspan measures up to 8 feet.

If you're brave enough, you can bungee jump from a road bridge that runs over the Zambezi river. Whoa!

The Falls have a permanent rainbow made by sunlight shining through the clouds of spray. On some nights, there is a "moonbow"—a rainbow caused by the light of the full moon.

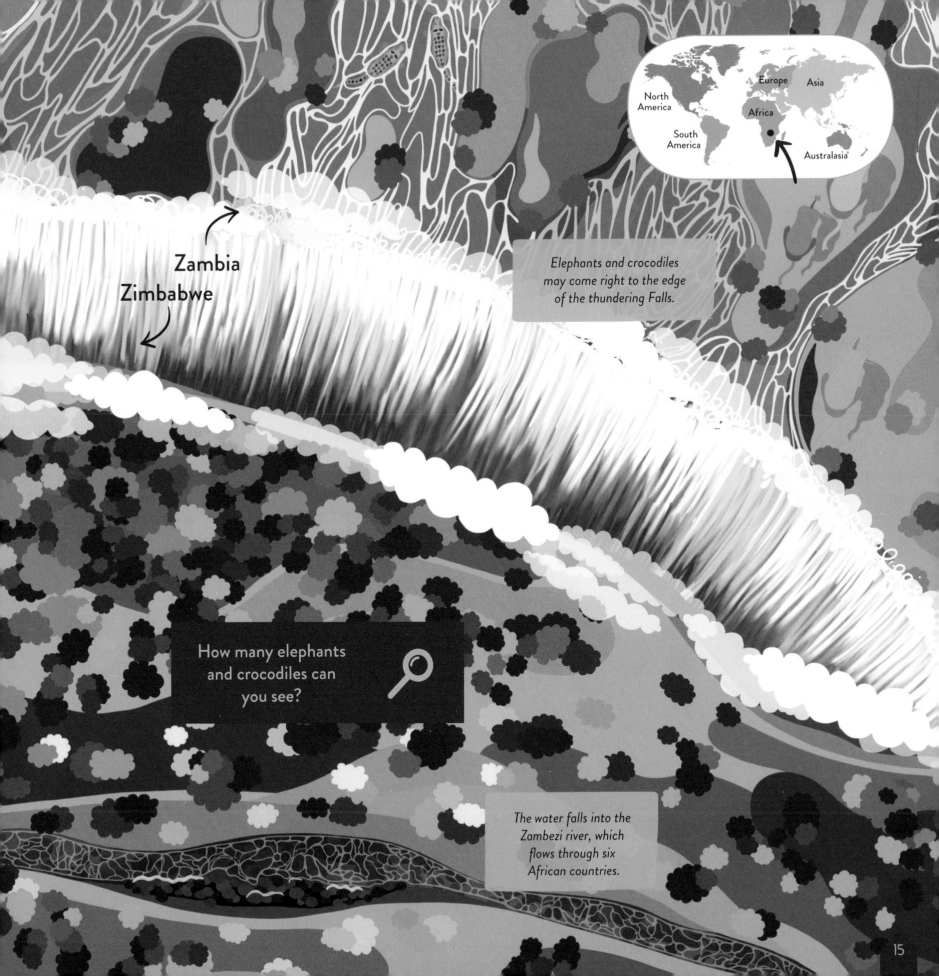

Zambia

Zimbabwe

Elephants and crocodiles may come right to the edge of the thundering Falls.

How many elephants and crocodiles can you see?

The water falls into the Zambezi river, which flows through six African countries.

North America

South America

Europe

Africa

Asia

Australasia

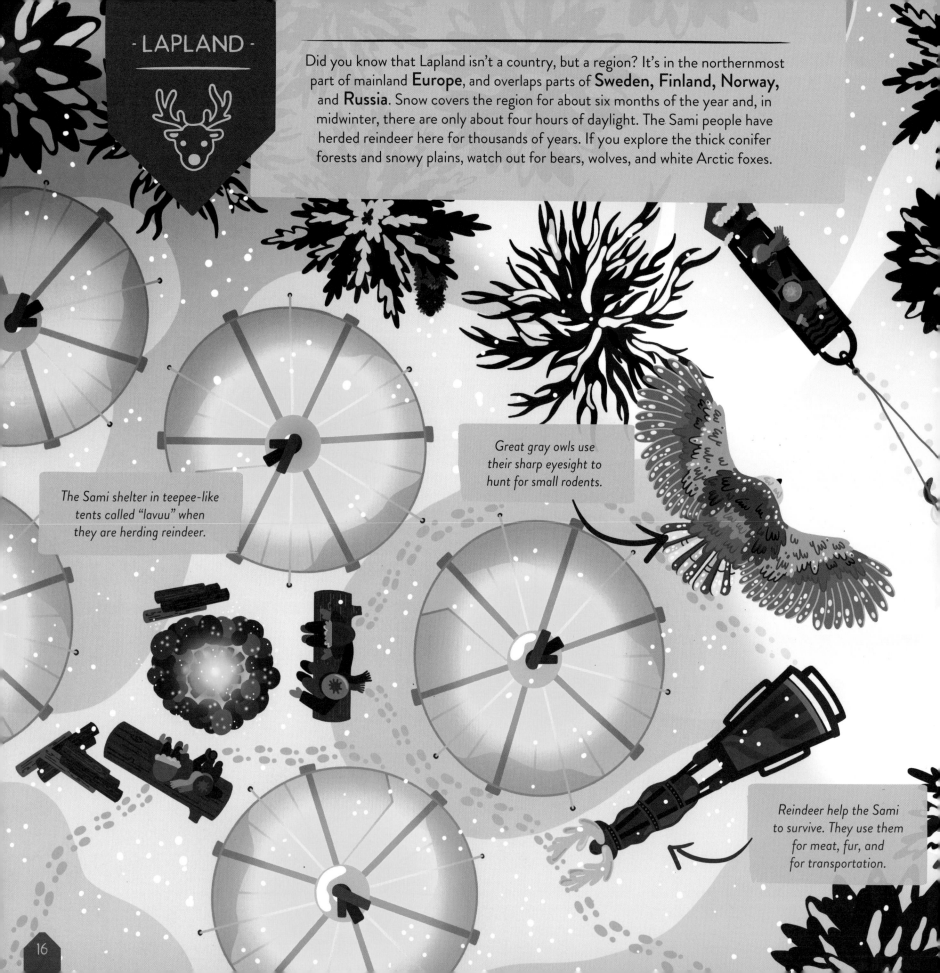

· LAPLAND ·

Did you know that Lapland isn't a country, but a region? It's in the northernmost part of mainland **Europe**, and overlaps parts of **Sweden, Finland, Norway,** and **Russia**. Snow covers the region for about six months of the year and, in midwinter, there are only about four hours of daylight. The Sami people have herded reindeer here for thousands of years. If you explore the thick conifer forests and snowy plains, watch out for bears, wolves, and white Arctic foxes.

Great gray owls use their sharp eyesight to hunt for small rodents.

The Sami shelter in teepee-like tents called "lavvu" when they are herding reindeer.

Reindeer help the Sami to survive. They use them for meat, fur, and for transportation.

Look closely at the picture. How many wolves can you see?

North America

South America

Europe

Africa

Asia

Australasia

A team of husky dogs pulls the sled that the Sami use to travel over the snow.

On a clear night, if you are lucky, you might see an awesome natural wonder in Lapland, called the Northern Lights. This is a series of glowing, flickering colors dancing in the sky. The display is caused by tiny particles streaming out of the Sun and hitting Earth's atmosphere.

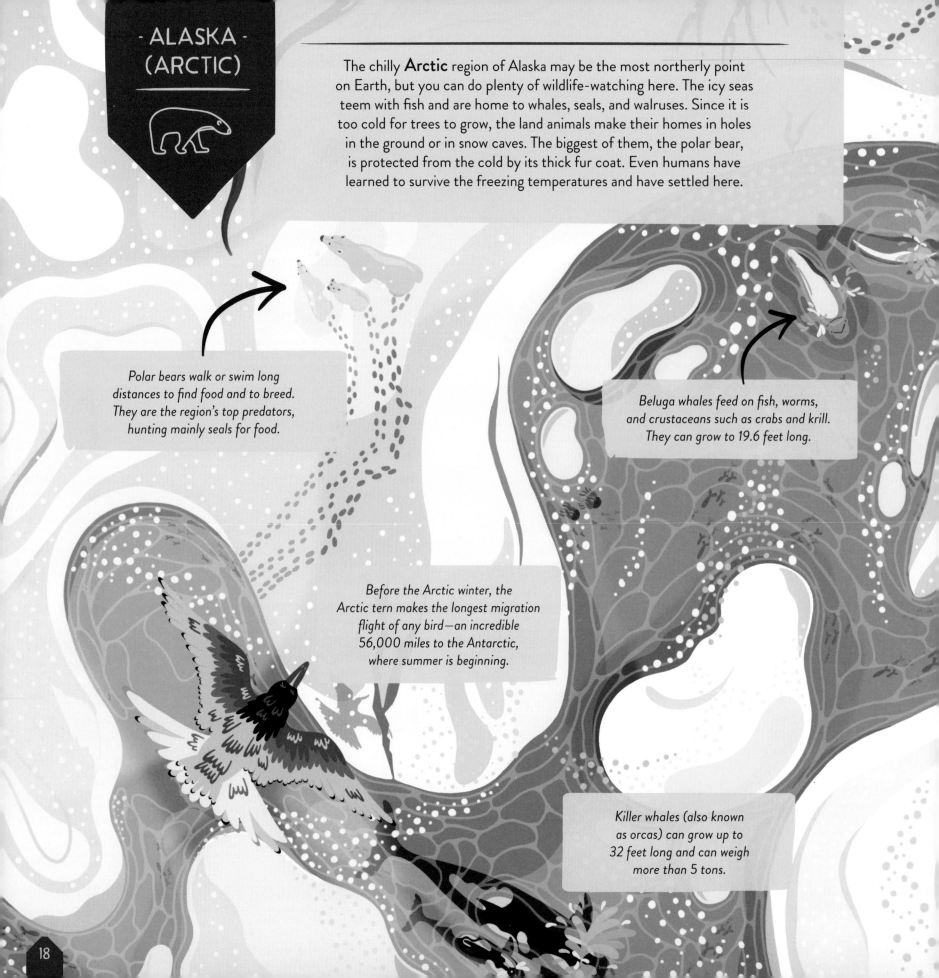

- ALASKA - (ARCTIC)

The chilly **Arctic** region of Alaska may be the most northerly point on Earth, but you can do plenty of wildlife-watching here. The icy seas teem with fish and are home to whales, seals, and walruses. Since it is too cold for trees to grow, the land animals make their homes in holes in the ground or in snow caves. The biggest of them, the polar bear, is protected from the cold by its thick fur coat. Even humans have learned to survive the freezing temperatures and have settled here.

Polar bears walk or swim long distances to find food and to breed. They are the region's top predators, hunting mainly seals for food.

Beluga whales feed on fish, worms, and crustaceans such as crabs and krill. They can grow to 19.6 feet long.

Before the Arctic winter, the Arctic tern makes the longest migration flight of any bird—an incredible 56,000 miles to the Antarctic, where summer is beginning.

Killer whales (also known as orcas) can grow up to 32 feet long and can weigh more than 5 tons.

North America

Europe   Asia

Africa

South America

Australasia

You can see walruses lying on the sea ice. A layer of blubber (fat) under the skin keeps them warm.

Look closely at the picture. How many Inuit people can you see?

The native people of the Arctic are called the Inuit. They have lived in this region for 4,000 years.

- MOUNT - EVEREST

These mountaineers are close to reaching the summit of Mount Everest, in the **Himalayas,** in **Asia.** At 29,029 feet, Everest is the highest mountain in the world. It will have taken the mountaineers about two months, in freezing subzero conditions, to climb this far. Up here above the clouds, the air has less oxygen, which makes breathing difficult. The climbers must battle snowstorms and sudden gusts of wind to reach the top.

Colorful prayer flags decorate Everest's summit. The Himalayan people believe that when the wind blows the flags, blessings and love are spread across the land.

Look closely at the picture. How many geese can you see?

The climbers wear helmets and warm clothing. They are roped together for safety, and each carries a backpack holding food, water, and oxygen.

Migrating flocks of bar-headed geese have been tracked flying at this extremely high altitude.

If you don't want to climb to the summit, you can view Mount Everest from a plane!

Everest is the tallest peak in the Himalayas. Several of Earth's highest mountains make up this mountain range, which is 1,491 miles long and crosses five countries.

North America

South America

Europe

Africa

Asia

Australasia

Lhotse

Everest

Makalu

Three Himalayan peaks

· HA LONG · BAY

This picturesque bay in northern **Vietnam** is dotted with nearly 2,000 rocky islands. Legend says that the bay was created by a family of dragons, sent by the gods to fight off invaders. The dragons spat out jewels and jade to form a wall, which turned into a string of islands jutting high above the water. Many of the islands are tree-covered and you can see animals such as monkeys, bats, and birds. People come to visit the islands and to swim and dive in the warm emerald-colored water.

Birds of prey called black kites swoop down to grab catfish from the crystal-clear waters.

If you snorkel in the bay, you can see coral reefs teeming with fish.

Look closely at the picture. How many different monkeys can you see?

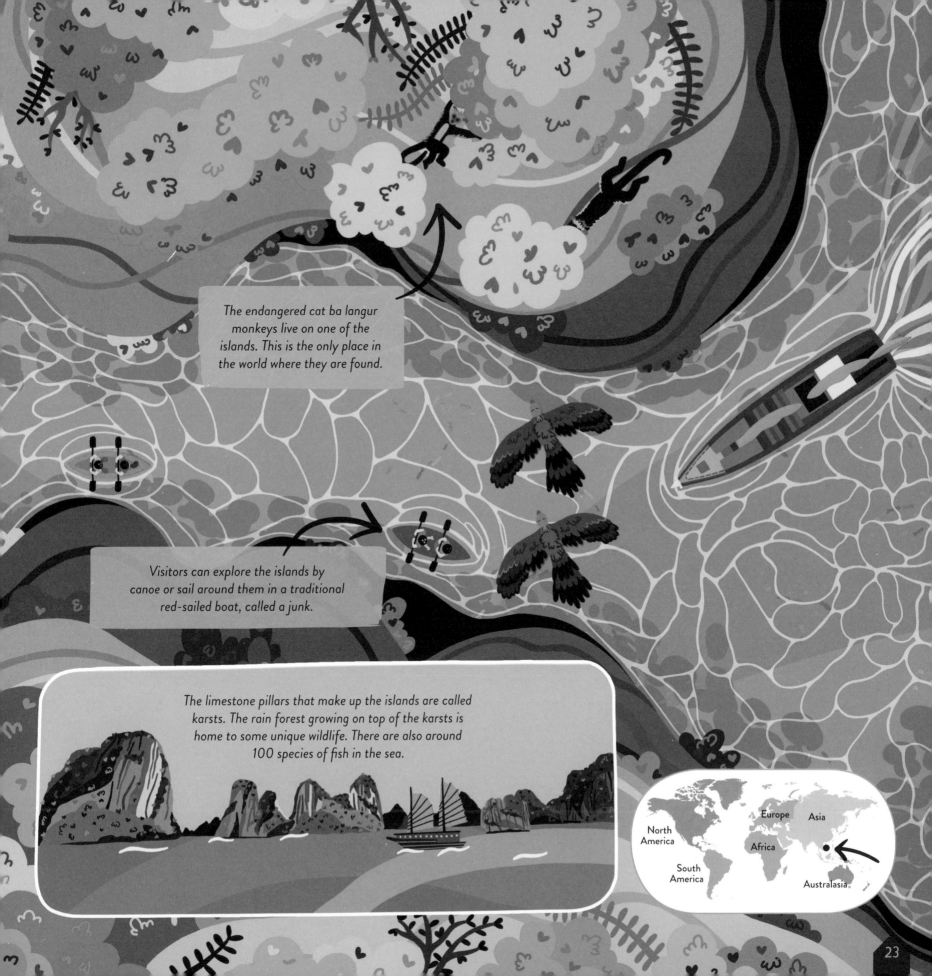

The endangered cat ba langur monkeys live on one of the islands. This is the only place in the world where they are found.

Visitors can explore the islands by canoe or sail around them in a traditional red-sailed boat, called a junk.

The limestone pillars that make up the islands are called karsts. The rain forest growing on top of the karsts is home to some unique wildlife. There are also around 100 species of fish in the sea.

North America

South America

Europe

Africa

Asia

Australasia

TENGGER CALDERA

The people in this picture are standing on the edge of a smoking volcanic crater, looking down inside it. The volcano is Mount Bromo, in **East Java, Indonesia**. This live volcano is one of five that make up a dramatic landform, the Tengger Caldera. To reach the steps leading to the top of Mount Bromo, you have to walk, drive, or even ride a pony across a flat, dusty landscape. It's an awesome experience—like being on the moon!

The Tengger Caldera volcano group is more than 800,000 years old. A vast area of sand, the Tengger Sand Sea, surrounds it.

The smoking crater bubbles with sulfur, which has a horrible smell—kind of like rotten eggs!

The besra sparrow hawk is a bird of prey that lives in this area. It hunts for lizards and small rodents.

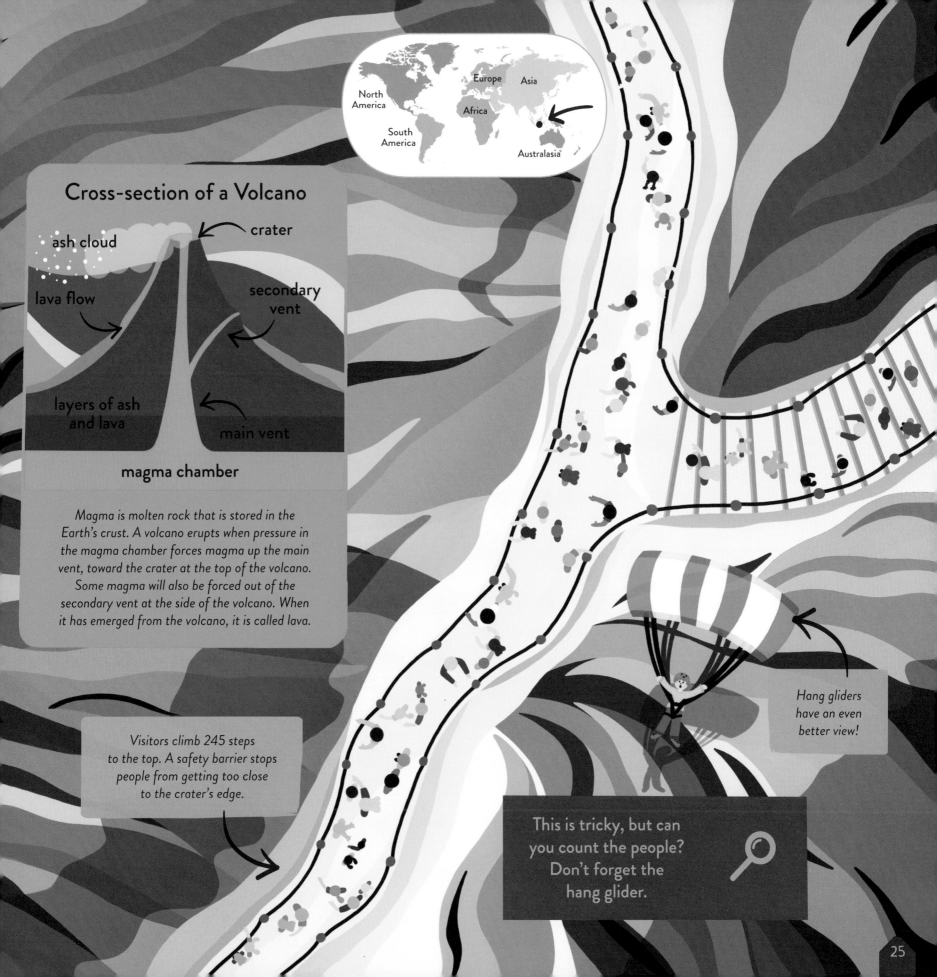

Cross-section of a Volcano

ash cloud

crater

lava flow

secondary vent

layers of ash and lava

main vent

magma chamber

Magma is molten rock that is stored in the Earth's crust. A volcano erupts when pressure in the magma chamber forces magma up the main vent, toward the crater at the top of the volcano. Some magma will also be forced out of the secondary vent at the side of the volcano. When it has emerged from the volcano, it is called lava.

North America

South America

Europe

Asia

Africa

Australasia

Visitors climb 245 steps to the top. A safety barrier stops people from getting too close to the crater's edge.

Hang gliders have an even better view!

This is tricky, but can you count the people? Don't forget the hang glider.

- LAKE - NAKURU

The hundreds of thousands of flamingos that feed on algae in Lake Nakuru National Park in **Kenya, East Africa**, make a stunning sight. The salty lake is quite small, but at times there are more than a million lesser flamingos here. When they are gathered in huge numbers, the lake seems to turn a beautiful pink color. A huge number of other bird species, including African fish eagles and pelicans, also visit the lake.

The pink color of the flamingos comes from the algae they eat. This contains beta carotene, which is also found in carrots. It gives the feathers their pink-red color.

This is a dream destination for wildlife watchers. Giraffes, rhinos, and hippos roam the shoreline. The surrounding wooded grassland is home to predators, such as lions, cheetahs, and leopards.

Fewer flamingos come to the lake to feed than before. This is due partly to changing water levels and partly due to pollution, caused by more visitors to the park.

The flamingos do not spend the whole year at Lake Nakuru. They go wherever they can find algae to eat, and sometimes migrate to other lakes in the area.

Look closely at the picture. Can you see a pelican among the flamingos?

27

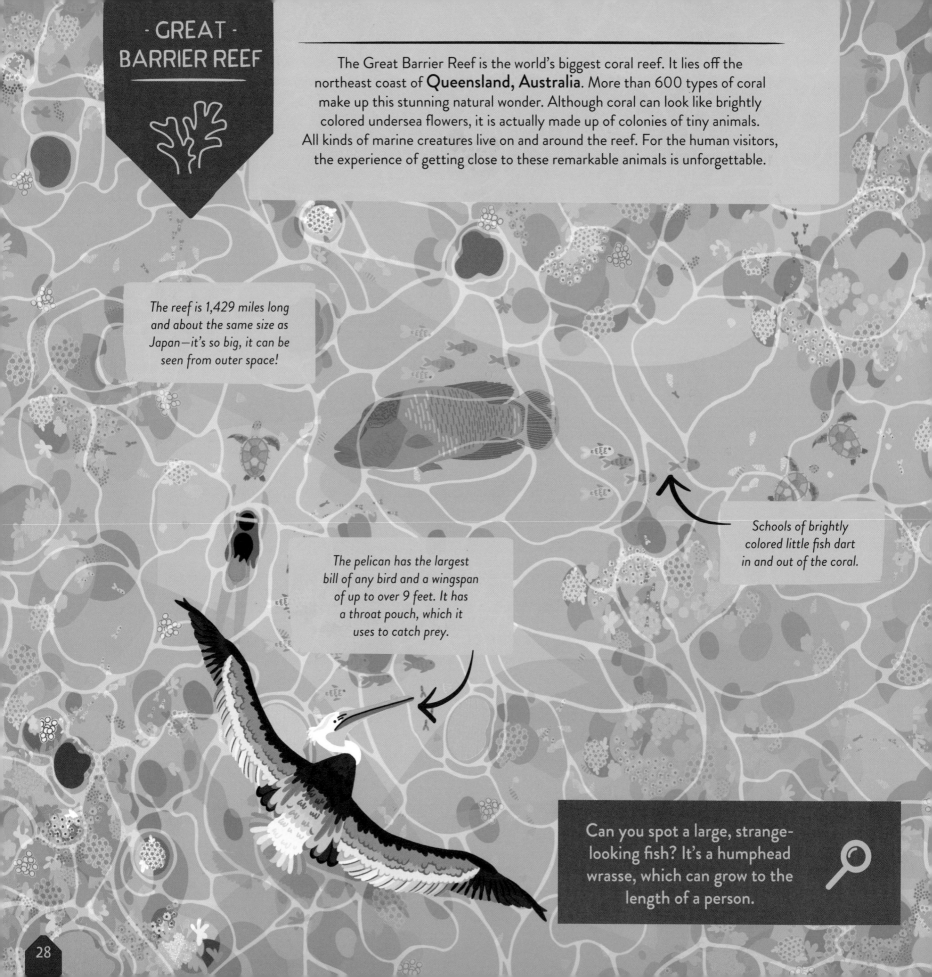

· GREAT · BARRIER REEF

The Great Barrier Reef is the world's biggest coral reef. It lies off the northeast coast of **Queensland, Australia**. More than 600 types of coral make up this stunning natural wonder. Although coral can look like brightly colored undersea flowers, it is actually made up of colonies of tiny animals. All kinds of marine creatures live on and around the reef. For the human visitors, the experience of getting close to these remarkable animals is unforgettable.

The reef is 1,429 miles long and about the same size as Japan—it's so big, it can be seen from outer space!

The pelican has the largest bill of any bird and a wingspan of up to over 9 feet. It has a throat pouch, which it uses to catch prey.

Schools of brightly colored little fish dart in and out of the coral.

Can you spot a large, strange-looking fish? It's a humphead wrasse, which can grow to the length of a person.

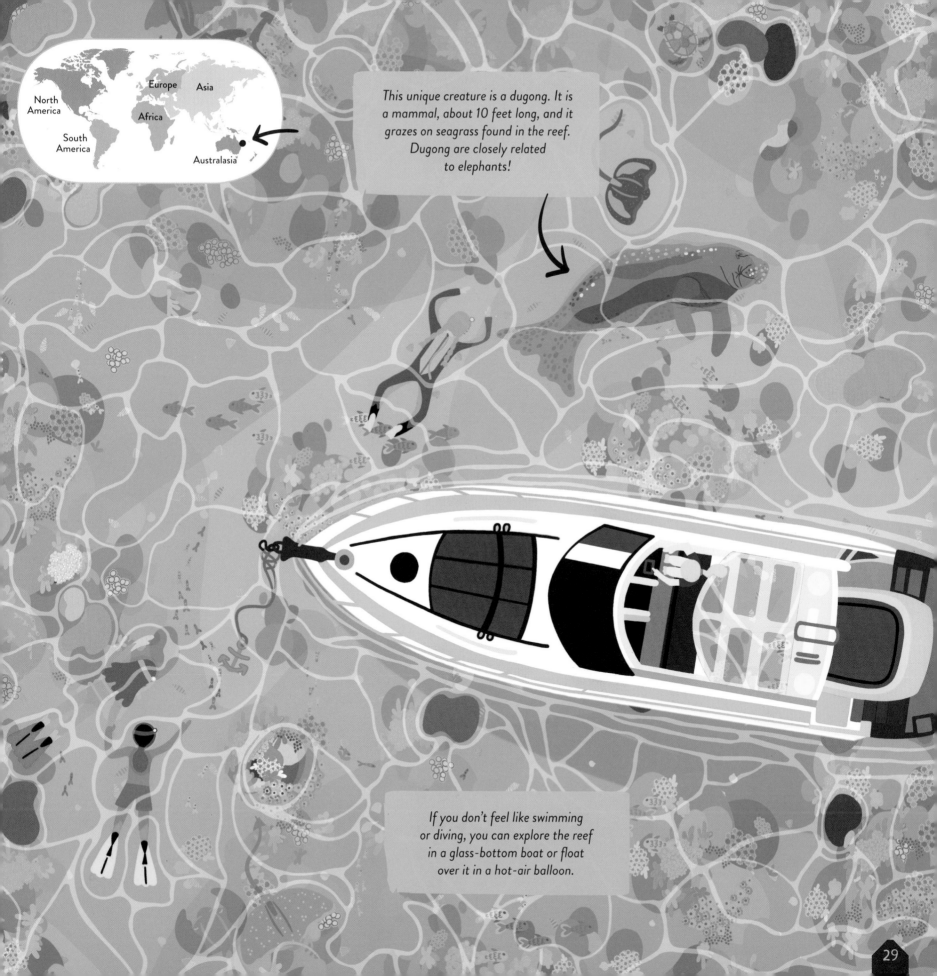

This unique creature is a dugong. It is a mammal, about 10 feet long, and it grazes on seagrass found in the reef. Dugong are closely related to elephants!

North America

South America

Europe

Asia

Africa

Australasia

If you don't feel like swimming or diving, you can explore the reef in a glass-bottom boat or float over it in a hot-air balloon.

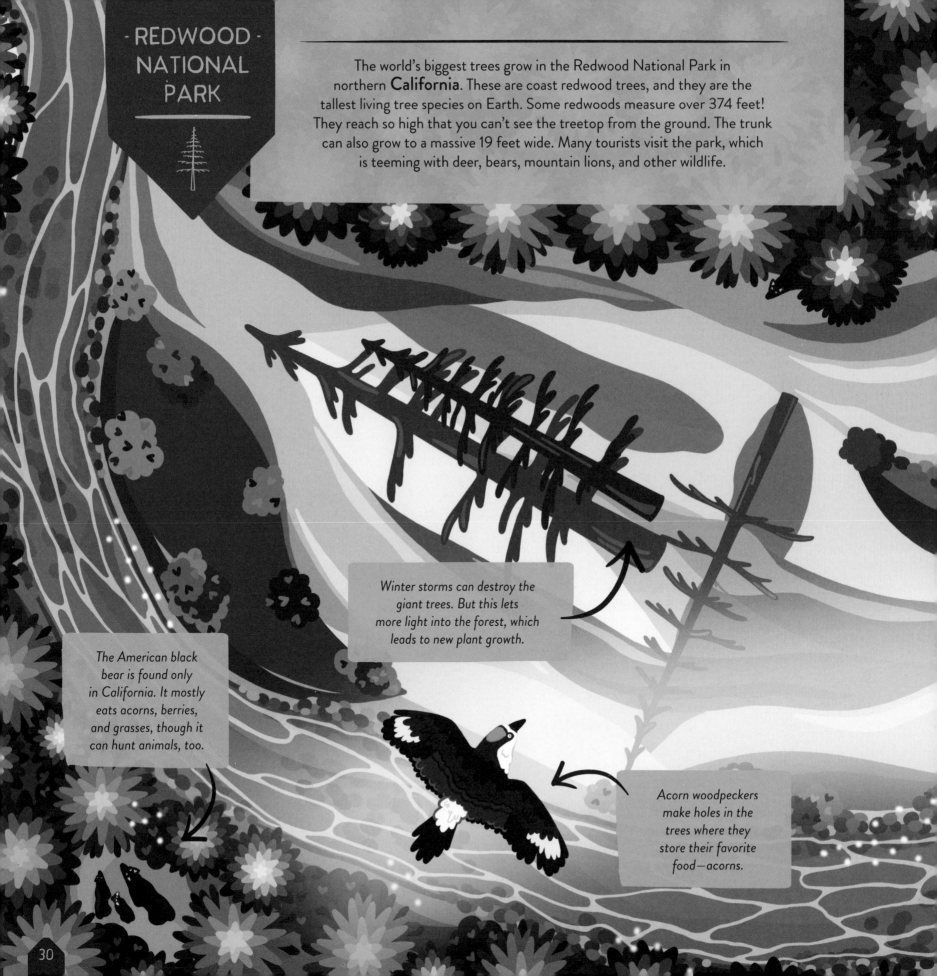

The world's biggest trees grow in the Redwood National Park in northern **California**. These are coast redwood trees, and they are the tallest living tree species on Earth. Some redwoods measure over 374 feet! They reach so high that you can't see the treetop from the ground. The trunk can also grow to a massive 19 feet wide. Many tourists visit the park, which is teeming with deer, bears, mountain lions, and other wildlife.

Winter storms can destroy the giant trees. But this lets more light into the forest, which leads to new plant growth.

The American black bear is found only in California. It mostly eats acorns, berries, and grasses, though it can hunt animals, too.

Acorn woodpeckers make holes in the trees where they store their favorite food—acorns.

Roosevelt elk roam the park. After moose, they are the second largest members of the deer family. Elk can run as fast as 35 miles per hour.

North America

South America

Europe

Asia

Africa

Australasia

The Statue of Liberty in New York is just over 300 feet tall. The largest known redwood tree, named Hyperion, measures 379 feet—that's a lot taller!

Look closely at the picture. How many bears can you see?

ANSWERS

pages 8–9
Eight boats.

pages 10–11
Fifteen zebras.

pages 14-15
Three elephants, two crocodiles.

pages 16–17
Three wolves.

pages 18–19
Three Inuit people.

pages 20–21
Ten geese.

pages 22–23
Three monkeys.

pages 24–25
Sixty-six, including the hang glider.

pages 26–27
The pelican is here!

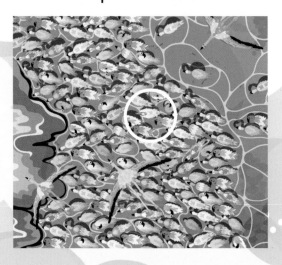

pages 28–29
This fish is the
humphead wrasse.

pages 30–31
Four bears.

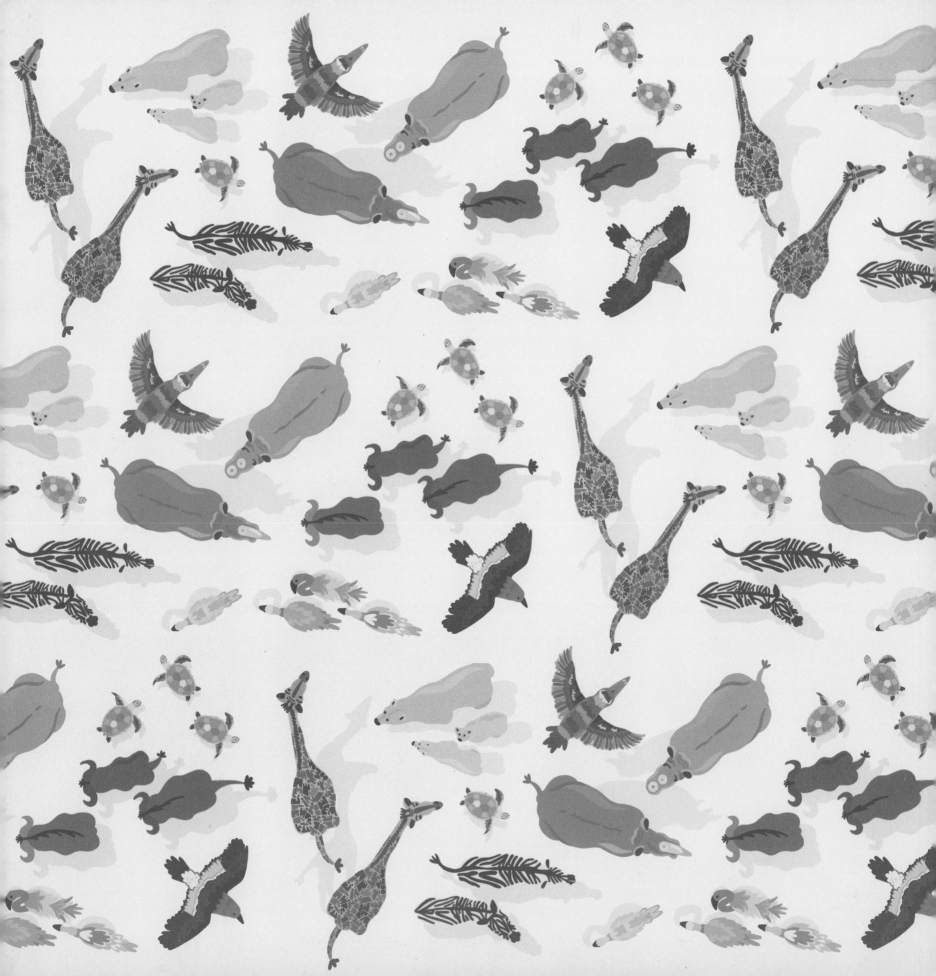